The Glory of God

Reflections from Exodus 33

The Glory of God

Reflections from Exodus 33

Lance Lambert

LANCE LAMBERT MINISTRIES

Richmond, Virginia, USA

Copyright © 2022
Lance Lambert Ministries
Richmond, VA
USA
All rights reserved

ISBN: 978-1-68389-121-5

www.lancelambert.org

Contents

Introduction 7
1. The Nature of Glory 9
2. Glory Through Sufferings 23
3. The House of My Glory 39
4. Seeing the Glory of God 57

Unless otherwise stated, all Scripture quotations are taken from the American Standard Version, with "Jehovah" changed to "the Lord" by the author.

Introduction

Lance shared a series of messages on the glory of God, focusing on the passage in Exodus 33 in his days at Halford House. The following chapters are taken from transcripts of these messages, edited only for clarity.

1.
The Nature of Glory

Exodus 33:17–18
And the Lord said unto Moses, I will do this thing also that thou hast spoken; for thou hast found favor in my sight, and I know thee by name. And he said, Show me, I pray thee, thy glory.

Show me, I pray Thee, Thy glory. This is an extraordinary thing. I have often stopped here after I had made the discovery that this happened after a tremendous amount of experience. Think of Moses' life, think of the way that the Lord met him in the burning bush and spoke with him out of the burning bush and said, "Take the shoes from off thy feet for the ground whereon thou standest is holy ground," and said, "My name is unspeakable. I Am that I Am, Jehovah." He revealed His name to Moses, and much else, and then sent him to Pharaoh. When you think of the way that Moses went in and out to Pharaoh, backwards and forwards all through the ten plagues, when you think of the Passover night, and all that happened in that tremendous deliverance on the Passover night when the angel of death went over, you would think that Moses had seen the glory of the Lord. You would think there was no need for him to say after so much experience, "Show me Thy glory."

You remember when he saw the pillar of cloud by day and the pillar of fire by night, which came between the children of Israel and their enemies, and which led them after the Passover, when they went down to the Red Sea, and the Red Sea opened. It was the pillar of fire that took its position behind them, and which came between them and Pharaoh's host. Then you think of all that happened in the wilderness. Years and years of genuine experience. They had manna from heaven every morning—by which they lived, and water out of the rock—a miracle every time it happened, and you think of the giving of the ten commandments. All this had taken place by Exodus 33. The ten commandments had been written with the finger of God! Moses had seen this miracle take place before his eyes. He had been shown the pattern of heavenly things in the tabernacle, all this had been revealed to him. This dwelling place of God, which Moses understood was but a symbol, a picture, a pattern of the divine reality, for which God sought more than anything else—the house of God, the dwelling place of God, the home of God—all this Moses had seen. Now here, in this 33rd chapter, he is having a talk with the Lord, and he has said to the Lord that if His presence does not go with them, then "do not carry us up hence". The Lord had said to him, "My presence shall go with thee, and I will give thee rest." Then Moses turns back again to the Lord and says, "Lord, show me Thy glory."

The Church is the Dwelling Place of God's Glory

Now, I wonder whether you and I, as those who have been redeemed through the grace of God, really realise to what God has called us. Have we just become little Christians that can sing a hymn, that can say our prayers, that can read the Bible? Have we become people who have just a knowledge of faith? Are we people, in fact, that can work miracles and signs and wonders? Are we a people who know that God can do it? Are we a people who know the power of God, the provision of God, the miraculous provision of God? We may know all those things and still not touch the heart of the matter. Dear, dear child of God, you and I have been saved that we might become the receptacle, the dwelling place of God's glory. Now what does that mean? Does it excite you? I fear sometimes it does not because we are often more thrilled with other things than the thought of glory.

What is glory? Glory is the presence of God in a completely full and committed way. When God commits Himself, it is glory! It is absolute glory. You will remember that it was the God of glory that appeared unto our father Abraham. It was that vision, perhaps imperfect, but that vision of eternal glory that apprehended Abraham and tore him away from the culture and the civilization of which he was part and made him go out into the desert, just to be what some have—in a rather deriding way—called him, "a wandering Bedouin." He was no wandering Bedouin. If he came here, his culture, his understanding, his education, his insight, and his perception would put us all to shame. He was so gripped by the God of glory who appeared to him that he went out into the desert and forgot Ur of the Chaldees and forgot all his education and background. He never ever obtained the land which had been promised, but he sought for the city which has the foundations, which we are told in the end will be the vessel of the glory of God. This matter of glory is something which really belongs to maturity.

Is There Something More?

Is it not an extraordinary fact that for you and me, as Christians, everything which is right and legitimate in the Christian life turns sour? Why? Everything in many ways, those things which we read, over which we are enthralled, in the end lose their gilt edges. We become used to them and familiar with them, and they do not satisfy anymore. Oh, how I see it as I move around, on all sides, all different kinds of Christians. Once they become familiar, once they become used to it, it is turned somehow to contempt in one way. They are thankful for what God has done, but they are all deeply conscious that "there is something more, there is something more, there is something more," and there is something more. That something more is summed up in the one word, glory. If you were to take a concordance, look up the word glory, and go through the whole Bible, you will be overwhelmed by the amount that is in the Word of God about glory. Moses certainly had enough experience to create two or three Bible colleges, run two or three theological courses, and start a healing campaign; I am also quite sure he could write a number of books of, "My Experience Through the Red Sea," or, "The Night I was in Egypt, when the Angel of Death Passed Over," or, "How I Saw Water Come Out of the Rock in the Desert." Oh, Moses could have done it all. However, at the end of it all, with all that behind him, he says to the Lord, "Show me Thy glory."

Now, why? Furthermore, the Lord does not answer him by saying, "Well, now Moses, I have shown you My glory. Did you not see Me when Sinai smoked with fire in a cloud? Did you not see Me in the pillar of cloud and fire? Did you not see Me in the burning bush?" The Lord never said that. He said to Moses, "I will." If you read the next few verses in Exodus 33, He said to Moses, "I will." "I will," He said, "I will put you on a rock, and when I pass by, I will hide you in a cleft of the rock, and I will put my hand over you, so that you will only see My back." In other words, glory is not an attribute. It is the person of God. It is the most intimate thing, the fundamental thing about His presence and His being. So intimate. So Him. God will not cheapen Himself by just exposing Himself to the gaze of any child of God. Or we can put it this way: the glory of God, the inner person of God, the actual presence of God is so powerful that it would destroy us. Even a redeemed child of God could be damaged if God exposed Himself too suddenly. We forget the statement, "Our God is a consuming fire" (Hebrews 12:29). Sometimes we feel we have seen something of the Lord, but we have touched only the fringes of His ways, the outskirts of His way. These are tremendous things when the Lord touches us, but it is only the fringe of His ways.

Experience Creates a Thirst for God

Now, do not just forget what I say, but really go back and look at this book of Exodus and you will find that what I have said is true. If you had the experience that Moses had, I am sure that you would feel that you are somebody. You would be sitting there in your seat saying, "Hmm, quite good. It is quite good what He is saying. Of course, I have had a lot of experience. I wish I could share it with him. It might help him." We are something! However, Moses was not like this. In other words, it leads me to say this, that whenever we have a genuine experience of God, we thirst for more. The more knowledge we have, the less knowledge we have got. That is true. The more we know, the more we know we do not know. The more experience we have, the greater the longing and desire in our hearts for something more. I cannot understand these people who say they have got everything! I just cannot understand them. As far as I can see, they must be dead fish. It just is not true to the Word of God. There is not a single person in the whole Word of God who was touched by God, that did not long for more. Do not come to me and say that the New Testament says that you have got it all. Of course you have got it all, but what about the apostle Paul? "I count all things but loss." "I press on," he says. Once God has apprehended you, once you have had genuine experience, an appetite is created, which will never be satisfied by anything here on Earth. Never. Never will it be satisfied, even by any spiritual experience here on Earth. Should anyone be seeking for something they think is going to be the end-all and be-all of everything down here, mark what

I say, never. It will only do something in you and carry you on with something more of God. For whatsoever the Lord doeth, it is forever. You will go on with something more done in you forever. It will in the end only create a greater capacity for Him. It creates a longing for Him, so that if you go on with the Lord, at the end of the journey, you will long for Him more than you ever did at the beginning. That is the work of grace through life to make us long for Him more and more and more and more. Well, that is Moses' experience.

Now, I am just quickly going to take you through a whole ramble through Scripture, hopefully say few comments on these verses, and hope that does the work. The Lord will do the rest. Now, listen to these words in 1 Peter 5:10, "And the God of all grace, who called you unto His eternal glory." Here you have eternal glory. That is the objective. Here also, you have the God of all grace. That is the means. How are you and I—unworthy, difficult, complex people—to be brought from the position we are in to eternal glory, the maximum of glory that God can work in us and for us? How? The God of all grace. I am so glad it says the God of all grace. It would have been lovely if it had said, "The God of all power," because we would need such power to change people like us, but I am even more glad that the Word of God says, "the God of all grace." That is deeper than even power. "The God of all grace, who called you unto His eternal glory in Christ," mark that, the eternal glory is in Christ, "… after that ye have suffered a little while, shall himself perfect, complete, establish, strengthen …" In other words, He will make you full, absolutely complete. He will establish, give you good roots, good foundations, and He will empower you, endue you with power, strengthen you. But you see what it says, you cannot get away from it, "… after that you have suffered a little while." That is what God thinks of this life down here, suffering a little while. We do not think like that. In actual fact, you know this life is just like the chrysalis stage of the butterfly. In God's sight, it is suffering a little while, then out we emerge into His eternal glory, called unto His eternal glory.

Now, if you turn back, you will find in Hebrews 2:9–11: "But we behold Him who hath been made a little lower than the angels, even Jesus, because of the suffering of death crowned with glory and honour, that by the grace of God He should taste of death for every man. For it became Him, for whom are all things, and through whom are all things, in bringing many sons unto glory, to make the author of their salvation perfect through sufferings. For both He that sanctifieth and they that are sanctified are all of one: for which cause He is not ashamed to call them brethren." Now let us look at that. He, that is Christ, is bringing many sons unto glory. He is not just bringing us to be people who can do wonderful things, people who can preach in a glorious way, people who can work in a marvellous way. All these things are so. These are right. However, God is supremely bringing us, by Christ, unto glory and He has made the author of our salvation perfect through sufferings. He that is sanctified, and they that are sanctified are all one. In other words, the God of all grace has laid a completely sure and certain foundation in the character and the finished work of the Lord Jesus Christ, to achieve glory for us, to bring us to glory.

The Provision

If you turn back to Hebrews 10:10–14, we have exactly the same thought again, "By which will we have been sanctified through the offering of the body of Jesus Christ once for all. And every priest indeed standeth day by day ministering and offering oftentimes the same sacrifices, the which can never take away sins: but He, when He had offered one sacrifice for sins for ever, sat down on the right hand of God; henceforth expecting till His enemies be made the footstool of His feet. For by one offering He hath perfected for ever them that are sanctified." Now, there is the most wonderful statement. It tells me that the Lord Jesus Christ has, by the one offering of Himself, perfected forever them that are sanctified. For everything that you and I need to bring us right through from sin to the presence of God, the glory of God has been provided. Everything you and I need in order to change—ugly, worthless, sinful, vile creatures such as you and me—into saints of God, into vessels of His glory has been achieved by the Lord Jesus Christ. It is all done. It is not as if God has got to do something more. It is done. The finished work of Christ has achieved it. Everything, everything, everything necessary for you and me personally, everything necessary for the building and completion of the Church, the house of God, the body of our Lord Jesus Christ, it has all been done. By one offering, He has perfected forever them that are sanctified. By now you may not feel that you are being perfected, but God in His grace and His mercy has already made all the provision for bringing many sons unto glory at every stage of the way. The provision is there. The God of all grace who hath called you unto eternal glory has made provision.

He has not said, "Now then all of you, come on. Start a race, and we will see how many fall out." There is a sense in which many do fall out. But the point is that they fall out because of unbelief, or sin that is not dealt with. The provision is there, and you can take it at every stage of the pilgrimage. There is no reason why any single person cannot become a vessel of His glory, or cannot become part of that city of God, which will be the eternal expression of His glory. It does not matter how worthless you are, how intricate, how complex, how awful your circumstances, how difficult your temperament and nature, how unbelieving by nature you are. God can do it. The provision is made through the finished work of the Lord Jesus, and through the outpoured Holy Spirit. That is why, dear child of God, the battle is just to stop us from taking what is ours. Isn't that the battle? We all know sometimes we are not what we should be. We all know as we read the Word that somehow there is not a correspondence. So, we run around in circles, and in our mind, the devil sort of whispers to us, "You need something more." That is right. You do need something more. But then he gets you onto the idea that, somehow, God has got to do something special for you, which has never been done before. It has all been done. The provision has been made. The secret is to take it. Oh, for eyes that could be open to just simply see this matter. It will change us. There is the provision. It is all there to be taken.

I will put it this way. Supposing you and I had lived in the days when we wandered in the wilderness as the people of God did for 40 years. Supposing you were starving. Now I say, "Now look here. What are you starving for?"

"I don't know, I feel so unworthy."

"Now look, the manna comes down every morning. It comes just down outside your tent flap, the flap door of your tent, just outside."

"Oh, no, no, no, no, I've never seen it."

"Don't be silly. I've seen it. I collect it outside my tent. Of course, I see yours there every morning not gathered."

"It's there every morning?"

"Provided every morning! The God of all grace has provided it."

"Oh, you see, no, He wouldn't speak to me. He wouldn't do it for me. Anyway, it was all done at the Passover."

"All right, then starve." You will die.

What can we do? You say it was all done at the Passover, well of course, it was all done at the Passover. The Passover lamb was the one who achieved everything, who brought everything, but you have got to go out and collect the manna. Suppose you said, "Oh, I am thirsty," and there was dear old Moses over there. He had just spoken to the rock and the water was flowing out. Suppose you say, "Oh, I am so thirsty. It is no good me going down there with all the others. It's no good." It is there. You have got to stoop down and drink humbly. Be one of the others, do not make yourself so special. Everyone seems to think, "I am a special case. I am more difficult than the others, and I have got a terrible background. I am a terribly difficult person anyway, and really, I am quite unique. I am quite unique. I mean, God has done it all for all the others but ..." It is only pride. Inverted pride, that is all. You think that you are somehow a special case. You are not a special case. The water is there. The manna is there; go and eat it. When the quail come and you want to change your diet,

The Nature of Glory

it is no good you saying, "None for me. None." They have dropped on the ground! Collect them! Collect them! They are there for you. God has brought them for you. Go out and collect them, the provision is there. It is all for you. You see what I mean? By one offering, one sacrifice of Himself, He hath perfected forever them that are sanctified. It is bringing you to glory. If you do not take that manna, if you do not drink that water, if you do not take those quail, you will die. You will become one of those odd, peculiar Christians, which are bound, who can talk and talk and talk about the day they heard C.H. Spurgeon, and the day they heard Moody, and the day this and the day that. They can open a biblical dictionary and tell you all of it and they can say, "Oh, it is marvellous, isn't it marvellous?" and it is as dead as doornails. They do not know a thing when it comes to practical experience, if a bomb dropped next door, they would not know how to pray. They just do not know what to do. That is all, it is as simple as that. It is experience that is required.

How do you get experience? Not by sitting on your haunches and saying, "It is done, it is done." Of course it is done. But experience is gained by appropriating what is done, and the consequences of what is done. Do you not realise that there are consequences because of the finished work of Christ? Do you not realise that everything has been given to you? Oh, I am not saying that you will not suffer. I am not saying that you will not go through dark times—but there is peace for you provided. There is life for you provided. There is joy for you provided. There is power for you provided. It is all provided. More importantly than even on the personal level, there is the building of the church. It is no good for us to just say, "Now, Lord, You said, 'I will build My church.'" The fact of the matter is that it is the olive trees emptying out gold from themselves that is the key. We can go on saying, "The Lord says, 'I will build my church, I will build my church,' oh, Lord, how glad we are that You are going to build Your church," and nothing happens. The church is just as unbuilt as ever until we see that there are consequences. The Lord has got to do the building through us, not apart from us, but through us and with us, and in us, and by us. That means sons of oil . Now, all this just comes down to one thing: that it is all done. So, the enemy's whole battle is to blind us to the provision in all kinds of ways. False theology. A sense of unworthiness. Introspection of the wrong kind. Or something that we are all, including myself, guilty of: taking out the binoculars and studying one another. Instead of looking at the tabernacle in the midst with the pillar of cloud and fire, we have got our binoculars well trained on the tents on either side of us. What is going on inside? What is happening in there? What are they like? What are they not like? Are they good enough and all the rest of it. All this means we do not see the provision. We do not take the provision, and we suffer.

Seeing the Inner Person of God

Well, that is the end of this ramble through Scripture. The point is that when you really go step-by-step through, it is extraordinary what there is in Scripture about glory. I would have liked to sit there much more. I think we have stopped where we ought to stop on the matter of the finished work of Christ. Christ is bringing many sons unto glory. We have no excuse. If one day there is no glory, we have no excuse. The provision is made. All we have to do is to take it, that is all, just take the Lord's provision and move ahead. I would like to have said very much more about the place of this glory, the habitation of this glory.

What is the reason why very few of us have ever seen the inner person of God? When a person has seen the inner person of God, they are never the same. Call it what you will. You can call it any experience you like, inner light, baptism of the Spirit, second blessing, sanctification. Call it what you will, but when a person sees the inner person of God, they are never the same. But why can't God do that more? Because the rock isn't under our feet. That is why. Even if it is, we have not been hidden in the cleft. That is why. Once God opens His heart to us and His inner person to us, we have to know as never before the foundation under our feet. We have to know as never before the security of Christ. We have to know as never before the covering, "I will cover thee with My hand." Do not think that to see the glory of God is a cheap or an easy thing, as far as God is concerned. It can happen in an instant. But, my dear friends, it means very much to God Himself. Well, may it be that into our hearts there comes a cry, "Show me Thy glory." It would not matter, dear child of God if you lived a whole lifetime, as long as before it is over you have seen the glory of God. Once you have seen that, you are apprehended for something more. You will not rest with the little things, all these other things on either side, and so on. They are all good, they are right, but you will never rest with them. Never. You are apprehended for that which I believe and know in my heart to be symbolised by the lampstand all of gold. It is the glory. It is the glory. It is a light to lighten the nations and you have got it. The glory of God did lighten the nations. There is no need of sun or moon or of light because the glory of God did lighten the nations and the Lamb is the lamp thereof. Who is the lampstand if it is not the city? Do you see? The glory! Oh, to reach it.

2.
Glory Through Sufferings

Exodus 16:10 says, "And it came to pass, as Aaron spake unto the whole congregation of the children of Israel, that they looked toward the wilderness, and, behold, the glory of the Lord appeared in the cloud." Then again, if you turn to Exodus 24:16–17, we read these words, "And the glory of the Lord abode upon mount Sinai, and the cloud covered it six days: and the seventh day he called unto Moses out of the midst of the cloud. And the appearance of the glory of the Lord was like devouring fire on the top of the mount in the eyes of the children of Israel. And Moses entered into the midst of the cloud." Now, that means that in actual fact, in one sense, we have a problem because it seems that Moses and the children of Israel had all beheld the glory of the Lord. So, why is it that Moses makes this a special request in Exodus 33:18, "Show me, I pray Thee, Thy glory," unless it means that there is, as it were, the outskirts of the Lord's ways. There is the fire, there is the appearance of the glory. There is the outward manifestation, as it were, the first thing that is apparent, the first thing that strikes you. Yet Moses knew that was not the fullness of glory. Glory was much more than just a fire that could be seen, glory was much more than a cloud that abode with a great smoke, like a great furnace upon Mount Sinai. Even when he entered into it and was encompassed by the cloud and the fire and the brightness, he knew that was not the fullness of glory, there was something deeper than all that.

Of course, we said previously that glory is probably the most difficult thing in the whole Bible to define. We sought to define it by saying it is the presence of God, as it were, just committed with complete satisfaction. It is the very being of God, it is not pomp and honour merely, sort of the blowing of trumpets and a great brass band, that kind of idea of glory. That may be just the outward show, the outskirts of it, the edges of it, if you like, the manifestation of it. But glory really is the committed presence of God, when He commits Himself to a people or to a person, fully and completely and eternally. That is glory. The immediate result is glory, everything is as it should be. Everything has a deep sense that this is as it ought to be. Therefore, because God is satisfied, we are satisfied. Because God has come into something, we have come into something. In other words, it is not that I am getting something for myself, but He is getting something for Himself. As He gets what He needs, and what He wants, so I get what I need and what I want. That is glory.

You will remember that we looked at a number of scriptures. We turned to 1 Peter 5:10, and we read and spoke about this verse, "And the God of all grace, who called you unto His eternal glory in Christ, after that ye have suffered a little while, shall Himself perfect, establish, strengthen you." Then we read the verse in Hebrews 2:9¬–10, "But we behold Him who hath been made a little lower than the angels, even Jesus, because of the suffering of death crowned with glory and honor, that by the grace of God He should taste of death for every man. For it became Him, for whom are all things, and through whom are all things, in bringing many sons unto glory, to make the author of their salvation perfect through sufferings." You remember we dwelt upon, at some length, the fact that the God of all grace has called you and me, us, to His eternal glory in Christ. The God of all grace. We dwelt upon the fact, in Hebrews 10, that the work that the Lord Jesus has done is a finished work. We particularly underline, "For by one offering He hath perfected them that are sanctified." In other words, everything necessary for bringing worthless, ugly, vile sinners such as you and me into the eternal glory in Christ has been done by the Lord Jesus Christ. The provision is all there. If we do not inherit the glory, if we are not finally filled with the glory of God, it is not God's fault. The provision is all there. Everything has been done on the basis, the foundation, of the finished work of the Lord Jesus Christ, and the outpoured Holy Spirit. Everything has been given to you and me.

Now, do mark the word in Hebrews 2:10 where it says, "in bringing many sons unto glory." The Lord is bringing us to glory. It is a process. He is bringing you and me to glory, and everything depends upon how you and I are ready to appropriate the provision that has been won for us by the Lord Jesus Christ on the cross, and made, as it were, effectual by the giving of the Holy Spirit. Therefore, if you and I do not know the cross, in all its aspects, we cannot know the glory of God. But I would like to say something more. If you and I do not know the Holy Spirit in all the aspects of His ministry and work, we cannot know the glory of God. Without the Holy Spirit, there is no glory. None whatsoever. It is impossible because the finished work of the Lord Jesus Christ must, of necessity, be a legal, theological matter. It is the Holy Spirit, who takes of the things of Christ and makes them real to us. It is He who not only makes real the purpose and objective of God, but He puts, as it were, the yearning in these sinful hearts of ours, the yearning for the glory of God.

You and I do not want glory. Let us face it, we do not really want God. How did most of us come to Christ? Was it because we loved God? No, but because in the mercy of God, He played on our selfishness. That is how you and I got there, let us face it. I have yet to meet the person who found the Lord because they loved Him. I found that everyone has been forced by fear, forced by circumstances, forced by emptiness, forced by aimlessness, forced by a fear of death or hell, forced by these things. We come to Christ; we flee to Him.

The Principle of Selflessness

Then God has to do a deep work in us whereby He turns us upside down, and gets rid of that self-centred principle, "I, I, I, I" all the time. He has got us into the salvation of God. Now He has to get us to a place where it is no longer, "I" but, "Christ" (see Galatians 2:20). That is why we have all the trouble. It is one trouble to get us to come to Christ, and believe me, the Lord has to drop a bomb on some of us before we are blown into the kingdom. It is the sovereign work of God to do it, but when He has done it, then, oh my, the dynamiting that has got to go on once we are there, to turn us over from this principle of unsaved human life: self. There is no glory where there is self-centredness. Just because a person is saved, it does not mean that they are not self-centred. Is not all the trouble in Christian work and all the trouble in the church, from this simple little thing of self? There it is. There is no glory where there is self.

First, turn to John 1:14. Now, here is the principle of selflessness. "And the Word became flesh and dwelt among us (and we beheld His glory, glory as of the only begotten from the Father), full of grace and truth." There you have it. The Word became flesh and dwelt among us. He forsook all. He laid His glory aside. That which was His rights and what he deserved, the position that was His, being on an equality with God, God the Son; He laid this all aside. So, John puts this little word in brackets, "and we beheld His glory." There was no selfishness in the Son. We beheld His glory. Glory, not of man, but glory as of the only begotten of the Father, full of grace and truth.

Now if you turn to II Corinthians 4:6, we read this. It is the same thing put in a slightly different way. "Seeing it is God, that said, Light shall shine out of darkness, who shined in our hearts, to give the light of the knowledge of the glory of God in the face of Jesus Christ." Think of it, the light of the knowledge of the glory of God in the face of Jesus Christ. Now, where are you going to see glory then, dear child of God? Are you going to see it in the devil? Of course not. Are you going to see it in this world? Of course not. Are you going to see it in the children of God? In one sense, of course not. Where must you look if you are going to see the glory of God? You must look into the face of Jesus Christ.

Look into the face of Jesus Christ. The light of the knowledge of the glory of God in the face of Jesus Christ.

The Son is Full of Glory

Do you want to know what glory is? My dear, dear friend, it is not just a matter of fire and smoke and thunder. It is not just, as it were, a great, divine firework display. Do you know that the Lord Jesus Christ always had the glory of God? When He was a carpenter, there He was working at His bench, glory as of the only begotten of the Father filling Him. Filling Him! Some people never saw it, but it was there. It was not manifested—that is where the fireworks come in. Glory is something much more essential than the outward expression. It is the very presence of God. It is the committed presence of God. There was the committed presence of God in human form, working at a carpenter's bench from sunrise to sunset, every day, dealing with difficult people, "This has not been made quite right. I said this should be done this way, it has been done that way." Probably they already said they changed their minds halfway and then blamed Him. Oh, I can just imagine all the difficult customers, clients and all the rest of it.

Don't you think the devil sent all the most difficult people in the whole district to Him? I am quite sure that the trial of the Lord must have been that the devil was trying to get Him down in every single way that was possible. I am sure the Lord probably had the most difficult clientele that any business ever had in the whole history of the world. But anyway, the fact is that it was glory. When you see the Lord Jesus throughout His life, no matter where you see Him there was glory. When He was sitting weary on the well, there was glory as of the only begotten of the Father. When he was indignant and made that scourge of cords and drove out those people from the temple saying, "You have made my Father's house a den of thieves and robbers," (Luke 19:46) it was glory! It was glory as of the only begotten of the Father. Yes, it was glory all the way through. When He wept at the tomb of Lazarus, (John 11:35) it was glory. When He burst into tears over Jerusalem, (Luke 19:41) it was the glory as of the only begotten of the Father. When in Gethsemane He sweat great drops of blood (Luke 22:44) —so terrible was the physical and mental pressure He went through, so that the angels had to come and minister to Him, otherwise He would never have lived to go to the cross—it was glory as of the only begotten of the Father. The greatest point of glory was when He was nailed to the cross. That was glory.

Now you see, dear friends, you and I have such a different idea of glory. We only think of the outward. The essential thing, the thing that matters is that which can carry a man through human life and into the most terrible hell on earth and out into the sunshine. Then there can be a spiritual display, a manifestation of the glory which will be forever. You and I know that it is not a superficial display. It comes from something within. It is a presence. It is a character. It is something worked into the very fabric of the being. Don't you see? Moses, in one sense, was a little tired of all the outward side. He had seen it all. He could write books, he could do a lot that you and I could not do. He was tired of that. He said, "Lord, show me Thy glory. It is the inward fulfilment, Lord, that I want, not just the outward. The outward, yes, but the outward will take care of itself." Get the inward, and in the end the outward will just flow out of it. So, you see, when you look at it, it is something tremendous. I mean, you turn over the pages to Hebrews 1:3 and what do we read? We read, "who being the effulgence of His glory, and the very image of His substance," there you are, the outshining, effulgence of God's glory. Now, my dear friends, we know where to look, do we not?

Vessels of Mercy, for His Glory

Now, having got that clear, let us start another little path. We go back to Romans 9:23, listen to this, "… and that He might make known the riches of His glory upon vessels of mercy, which He afore prepared unto glory." Isn't that wonderful? Vessels of mercy. Are you a vessel of mercy? Well, dear child of God, if you do not know that you are a vessel of mercy now, the longer you live and the nearer you get to God, the more you will know that you are a vessel of mercy. In other words, it was the mercy of God that created the vessel. You are a vessel of mercy; you do not deserve this mercy. We have given God every single right to forsake us, but you and I are vessels of mercy. Why are we these vessels of mercy? God does not just show His mercy to us in a condescending way, as if He is going to say, "Now, I want you all forever after to be crawling around on the floor, grovelling at My feet sort of saying, 'Oh, oh be merciful to us miserable sinners!'" But listen to it, "… that He might make known the riches of His glory, upon vessels of mercy afore prepared unto glory." When God made you a vessel of mercy, when He took hold of you, the whole idea was glory. Glory. What is glory? Glory is that God should commit Himself to you, not just for a touch, not just for a visit, but as His home. So, when you go on from Romans 9:23, we turn over to a very well-known scripture in Colossians 1:27. Listen to this "… to whom God was pleased to make known what is the riches of the glory of this mystery among the Gentiles, which is Christ in you, the hope of glory." Is Christ in you? If He is in you, there is a hope of glory. There is the certain hope of glory.

Now, I take it a further step. How much of Christ is there in you? If there is a little of Christ, there is a little glory forever. If there is more of Christ, there is more glory forever. If you are full of Christ, you will be full of glory forever. Do not think that God, who is the Master Craftsman, the Master Workman will give you too much rope. Do not think He will let you enjoy things too much in such a way that you are not prepared for the chiselling, the facing work, the breaking work, the work that He must do to make vessels of mercy prepared. You know, we have got this self-instinct so deeply inwrought into our very being that it is the hardest thing in the world for it to be touched. We would be happy to have anything else touched, even our money, anything. Yet, it is true, we would be prepared to give money rather than to have that self-life touched. You know the extraordinary thing, even grown-up Christians, more adult Christians (I do not mean physically, but spiritually) oh, what a fear there is about that self. Do you know, dear child of God, many of our fears about the work of the Holy Spirit are wholly over this? We are so afraid that once we really commit ourselves to the Lord in this way, He might start to tamper with us too much. We start to think, "I will have to do this, and this, and this, and this. This might have to be cleared up, that might have to be cleared, I might have to go that way." So, we become fearful.

Well, now, all right, all right. You see the Lord is a very ... well I was going to say He is a good psychologist in this way. He does not say, "Now, then you do it or else." He does not say that at all. He says, "Alright then, if you don't want your self-life touched, alright. I have saved you. Enjoy yourself. Go on, enjoy yourself." Of course, you go away, and you do not enjoy yourself. A good psychologist! You do not enjoy anything. You just go away, and you go into a deep sulk, "You know, it is all so hard". You blame everyone, blame Him, and blame everything, but in actual fact, the Lord says, "Now, look here, you don't want your self-life touched, all right. I am not going to touch you. I have saved you, and I will keep you, and I will bless you, and I will give you all kinds of things and you will have a riot of a time if you want it. But if you do not want your self-life touched, alright." Know that you can stop at any single point in the Christian life. You can stop. You can be a grown-up Christian who has gone a long way and then suddenly you say, "Nope, no more." It is alright with the Lord. He says, "I will leave you alone. You have got a lot, I will bless you, I will keep you, I will preserve you." But don't you ever come back to the Lord and say, "What about the glory?" One day when you are standing there and looking at someone, and you are thinking, "Oh, that glory, why haven't I got as much glory?" Just you remember, you were prepared for the cross. Christ in you is the hope of glory.

Therefore, you see, you and I have to be prepared for the price. There is no way around it, I mean, you only have to take your

Bible and start to read it in the light of what I have said and you will find it is true. If we suffer with Him, we shall reign with Him. It is certainly true. There is an "if." There is an "if." So, if you and I are prepared for the way, then alright, once we commit ourselves to the Lord, we do go through dark times sometimes, and we do go a strange way, but the end is glory. Now, never forget that. Christ in you, the hope of glory. What are the riches of the glory of this mystery? Christ in you, the hope of glory.

Let us look at II Corinthians 3:18. Now listen to this: "… but we all, with unveiled face beholding as in a mirror the glory of the Lord, are transformed into the same image from glory to glory, even as from the Lord the Spirit." Oh, what a word this is. Just think, just think. You say to me, "Alright then, there has to be more of Christ. There has to be more of Christ in my heart, in my life. How can there be more of Christ?" Well, here we have it, "… we all with unveiled face …" Have you got a veil on your face? Have you? Are there some things you do not want to see, or has the Lord done away with the veil? We all with unveiled face beholding as in a mirror the glory of the Lord. Imperfectly, but we have our eyes on Christ, who is the glory of God, the effulgence of His glory.

Transformed from Glory to Glory

Now then, what happens? We are transformed into the same image from glory to glory. Now, dear child of God, isn't that true? Whenever you and I catch a glimpse of Christ, if we are children of God, there is a deep yearning within. Now, I know this from my experience, and I know I have seen it again and again in others. The surest sign a person is born of God is that though they may be the most hopeless case in every single way, when they catch a glimpse of Christ, when somehow there is a season where the Lord, as it were, reveals Himself, there is a yearning in them. You want to be changed. You see, you are beholding as in a mirror the glory of the Lord.

Oh dear, when we start looking at one another ... we become so disillusioned and disappointed, we give up altogether. We think, "Oh dear, it is so awful, so terrible," but when we look at the glory of the Lord, a yearning comes, and we are transformed. We are ready to be obedient. You cannot force a person to be obedient, really, because that is not the obedience that God wants, that is the whole point. He does not just wield a big stick. But when it comes from within, then there is something that God responds to. Now it is, we are transformed into the same image from glory to glory. In other words, from one capacity of glory to a greater capacity of glory. Do you understand? This is what happened to the Lord Jesus. All the time, His capacity for the glory was being enlarged through suffering. You and I would have never noticed it, but He went through into that trial and out, from glory to glory. Then from this trial to that trial, from glory to glory. One day, all that is going to come into its own. Dear child of God, everything you have gone through, where you have been obedient to the Lord and really gone through, has been from glory to glory. You may not know it now, but one day you will and, oh, how thankful you will be. You will be so thankful.

The Spirit of Glory

I shall just give you two more references and leave it. I am only just taking one or two verses on glory out of a tremendous number, but the first is 1 Peter 4:14: "If ye are reproached for the name of Christ, blessed are ye; because the Spirit of glory and the Spirit of God resteth upon you." Now, that is a really beautiful word: resteth or tabernacleth. You go through with the Lord in this matter, and the Spirit of glory resteth upon you. The Holy Spirit is the Spirit of glory, the angel of the Lord's presence, the Shekinah glory. The Spirit of glory and of God. It is the ministry of the Holy Spirit, and the object of the Holy Spirit to practically get us to glory. He is the one who is taking us from glory to glory. He is the One who is enlarging the capacity, who is bringing more of Christ into us all the time. The Spirit of glory.

Peter writes here in 1 Peter to suffering saints who are being reproached, persecuted. He says, "Now then, you feel you have lost everything," such as, I think, hardly any of us in this room have known. They had lost their little ones. They had lost their home. They had lost their freedom. They had lost their reputation. They had lost their career. They had lost everything, and do you know how Peter comforts them? He says, "Be happy." What a thing to say. "Be happy," he says. "If you are reproached, if all this happens to you, this trial by fire … be happy. The Spirit of glory rests on you." My dear friend, when I heard brother Kaung speaking about those saints in China—why, you see, it may seem trite for us to say, "Be happy," but from God's point of view, it is true. They are the blessed ones, not us, for the Spirit of glory and of God tabernacles upon them. Something is being done which one day will all come into its own.

Power to Endure

My last verse is back in II Corinthians 4:17, and this is the cross at work. The Spirit of glory—yet here is the cross, "For our light affliction, which is for the moment, worketh for us more and more exceedingly an eternal weight of glory." Now, my dear friend, this light affliction, which is for a moment, for some of us it seems to be a lifetime. It never leaves us. It never leaves us. Yet, the Scripture says, our light affliction, which is for a moment. Well, if you look at it from down here, of course, it is a lifetime of affliction. You think, "Is it worth it?" but if you look at it from above, it is light affliction, which is for a moment. Doesn't the Word here in the next verse say, "… while we look not at the things which are seen, but at the things which are not seen: for the things which are seen are temporal; but the things which are not seen are eternal"?

Now if you look back in this chapter you will find verse seven, "… but we have this treasure in earthen vessels, that the exceeding greatness of the power may be of God, and not from ourselves." Now, please will you mark the word power? "… but we have this treasure in earthen vessels that the exceeding greatness of the power may be of God …" Where is this power? It is not always manifest. Read on, and well, do you think this kind of power means that you are authoritative? Dogmatic? Absolutely clear? Full of energy? You can blast anything and anyone? But listen to it. Listen to it, "… that the exceeding greatness of the power may be of God, not from ourselves; we are pressed on every side, yet not straitened; perplexed, yet not unto despair; pursued, yet not forsaken; smitten down, yet not destroyed" (II Corinthians 4:8–9). Oh, there is a different kind of power there. We need power which is visible sometimes, but this is the power that lasts, that kind of power when someone knocks you down and almost out, but, lo and behold, you are back again. Smitten down, yet not destroyed. Isn't that wonderful? It is completely true. The enemy goes, "Whomp!" and we are out. Just like the apostle Paul when he was taken for dead, stoned and taken for dead. They gathered around him and up he got. That is it.

Perplexed—should a Christian be perplexed? No mature Christians are perplexed who do not know the cross. If you know the cross, then you will know what it is to be perplexed. You see, the Lord breaks you like Jacob. You are crippled. You cannot walk like you used to walk, you are leaning, you are dependent. So, you see, it comes to pass, really, what the prophet Isaiah said, "… the lame shall take the prey," (Isaiah 33:23b). Isn't that wonderful? Who, in the end, will possess the glory? Who, in the end, will be filled with the glory? The prophet Isaiah saw it all in a few words, "… the lame shall take the prey." Well, are you prepared for that kind of work? The God of all grace who hath called you into His eternal glory in Christ, after that ye hath suffered a little while, Himself strengthen, establish, and perfect you (see I Peter 5:10). Glory.

Well, I have got a lot more to say about glory because it does not stay on the personal level, but we are going to leave it for now. It does not stay on the personal level. In fact, it is not a personal thing at all, in one sense. It is all to do with a corporate vessel in the last analysis, but practically, it comes down to you and me and what we are prepared for. Are you prepared for this? Am I prepared for it? Is there a veil over your face? Are we ready for the Spirit of glory to rest upon us and the cross to do its work? There will be glory and more glory and more glory.

Shall we pray?

Dear Lord, once we have really come to Thee, once Thou hast really taken hold of us, Thou must implant in our hearts a yearning for Thyself. Sometimes, it is submerged Lord in worldliness and sin and unbelief, but Lord, if Thy Spirit has ever really done anything in us, there is a yearning, deep, deep down in each of our hearts. Oh, Lord, we could put it all into those words and say, Lord, we want Thy committed presence. We want Thee to be in us, not just to know things, not even to be able to do things, not just to marvel at so many outward things. Have all that, Lord, yes, but more than that, to have Thyself dwelling within us, committed to us. Lord, then we would say with Moses of old, "Show me now Thy glory." We ask it in the name of our Lord Jesus Christ. Amen

3.
The House of My Glory

You will remember that we began in Exodus 33:18 where Moses said, "Show me, I pray Thee, Thy glory." The thing I sought to point out is that Moses made this request when, in fact, he had seen more than most children of God. He had seen the most extraordinary things. He had been a man who had acted in faith, and had seen the mighty works of God again and again and again. Furthermore, the most extraordinary fact that I pointed out last week, was that the glory of God had appeared twice already and the children of Israel had seen it and so had Moses. In one instance, Moses actually entered into the cloud of the glory of God. So, it is quite clear that Moses realised that glory was more than the outward manifestation. It was more than the fire, more than just the light, more than just the act. It was the committed presence of God Himself. The more Moses saw, the more he was involved, the more God used him, and the more he became aware of his own frailty and weakness, the more there came into him a quenchless yearning. A desire that was born of the Spirit of God, and which seemed, I suppose, in the end, to envelop the man. It is contained in this simple little question, "Show me, I pray Thee, Thy glory."

It is a very blessed thing, I believe, as a Christian, to be brought so far that suddenly we have within us, born of the Spirit of God, a yearning which will never be satisfied until we stand before God's face. Thank God for every time He meets us, and every time He fills us. Thank God for every experience we have of His fulness, but oh, to be preserved from those people who know they are full. To be preserved from an experience, which makes us, as it were, proof against the sweet and gentle, gracious workings of God's Holy Spirit, so that we feel we have it all, and that all we have to do is to tell others, or we have it in such a way that if we lose it, we just have to get it again like some kind of drug. No, dear child of God. That is not Christian maturity. That is not spiritual maturity. Spiritual maturity, is when a man gets to the place that Moses reached and there is nothing else that will satisfy the yearning in his heart, but only the glory of God. In other words, the committed presence of God. That committed intimacy of God where He dwells forever in us.

Well, now, we must say no more about that. What I want to do now is to take another line in this matter of glory, again a ramble through Scripture as we sought to do previously. Now, the whole point I want to say is this, that whilst the glory of God is fundamentally, to begin with, a personal thing, it is not a personal thing in its objective. In other words, each one of us must be transformed into the same image as the Lord from glory to glory. That is a personal thing. God does not do it in a mass production line. He takes you and me into different circumstances in different ways. He takes us from experience to experience, point to point, from glory to glory, from a smaller capacity for glory to a greater capacity for glory. He is enlarging us. He is bringing Christ into us. He is increasing Christ and every time there is something more of Christ, it is glory. We will not feel it down here, but one day, all that has been worked in us through the years will be glorified. It will not be the husks of our old man. It will not be the wood and the hay and the stubble of our old flesh, of the old creation, but everything of Christ that God has put into us however small will be the capacity for glory, the committed presence of God in its full and final manifestation.

The House of My Glory

Now if you turn to Isaiah 60:7b we read these wonderful words, "and I will glorify the house of my glory." I will glorify the house of My glory. Here then is our theme for our ramble through the Word at this time, "The house of My glory." I will glorify the house of My glory. You do not have to look far in the Word of God to find that glory is intimately and directly related to the temple of God, to the house of God, to the dwelling place of God, to the home or habitation of God. Wherever you look, you will find that glory is not just a personal thing. The glory of God finds its resting place, its dwelling place, its vehicle of manifestation in a house, in the temple. We know that the temple is a temple not made by human hands, but is eternal in the heavens. It is the body of our Lord Jesus Christ. We who are the living stones have been quarried out of the rock which is Christ and are being built together for a habitation of God in the Spirit. That is what it says in Ephesians 2:20–22. We are being built together as the whole building grows, its several parts growing together into a habitation for God in the spirit. "The house of My glory. "I will glorify the house of My glory," (Isaiah 60:7b).

Radiant

Look at this chapter, verse one, and listen to it, "Arise, shine; for thy light is come, and the glory of the Lord is risen upon thee. For, behold, darkness shall cover the earth, and gross darkness the peoples; but the Lord will arise upon thee, and his glory shall be seen upon thee." His glory shall be seen upon thee. To whom does the Lord speak? Well, He speaks to His people and these words were fulfilled in our Lord Jesus Christ! He is the one who shall "lift up His eyes round about and see; they all gather themselves together, they come to thee; thy sons shall come from far, and thy daughters shall be carried in the arms. Then thou shalt see and be radiant" (verse 4 and 5a). It is of the Lord Jesus that it is speaking, but of course, the Lord Jesus is the head of the church, and we are the body. The head and the body belong to each other. So these words are not only about our Lord Jesus, and are fulfilled in the person of our Lord Jesus and in His work, but they are fulfilled in us who have believed on Him and have been joined by the Spirit of God to Him.

The Place of My Feet–Glorious

So it goes on. In verse seven, "I will glorify the house of My glory." This is the house of My glory, these people are the house of My glory. I will glorify the house of My glory. Verse 13: "The glory of

Lebanon shall come unto thee, the fir-tree, the pine, and the box-tree together, to beautify the place of my sanctuary; and ..." listen to it, what an extraordinary statement, "I will make the place of my feet glorious." What an extraordinary statement. "I will make the place of My feet glorious." If you look at yourself, now dear friend, some of us have large feet and some of us have small feet but even the largest feet do not take up a large amount of space. What an extraordinary statement, "I will make the place of my feet glorious." It is not extraordinary when you think of it as our Lord Jesus. He is the glorified head. He will make the place of the feet of the body glorious—the whole, the whole work—all of it He will glorify, head and body. The Lord Jesus has gone into heaven as the earnest of glory. He has gone into heaven as the author, the captain, the pioneer, the file leader of our salvation, who is bringing many sons unto glory. He says, "I will make the place of my feet glorious;" not only will the head be filled with glory, and glorified, but the place of the feet shall be made glorious.

The Lord is Your Light–Glory

Verse 19: "The sun shall be no more thy light by day, neither for brightness shall the moon give light unto thee but the Lord will be unto thee an everlasting light, and thy God thy glory. There you have, I think, the closest thing to a definition of glory, "thy God thy glory," the committed presence of God. Verse 21: "Thy people also shall be all righteous, they shall inherit the land forever, the branch of my planting, the work of my hands that I may be glorified." If you read on forgetting the chapter division, you read that it is about the Lord Jesus, "the Spirit of the Lord is upon me because the Lord hath anointed me to preach good tidings unto the meek he hath sent me to bind up the brokenhearted, to proclaim liberty to the captives, and the opening of the prison to them that are bound," (Isaiah 61:1) and so on and so on. The last part of verse three: "That He may be glorified."

If you start now to look through Scripture, in the light of this, all kinds of things begin to fall into place. Turn back to Isaiah 43 and now, listen to this wonderful word again. Verses 5–7, "Fear not; for I am with thee: I will bring thy seed from the east, and gather thee from the west; I will say to the north, Give up; and to the south, Keep not back; bring my sons from far, and my daughters from the end of the earth; every one that is called by my name, and whom I have created for my glory, whom I have formed, yea, whom I have made." Now, you see, although it in one sense is personal—"everyone whom I have formed for My glory" —it is also corporate. They come from every side from east, from north, from south, from west they come from all sides. His sons and His daughters, every one that He has formed for His glory. You turn over the page to verse 21. Last part of verse 20: "To give drink to my people, my chosen, the people which I formed for myself, that they might show forth my praise." There you are; everyone that I have formed for My glory, the people that I have formed that they might show forth My praise. Oh what a glorious calling is ours.

Paul's Glory Writings

No wonder Paul, as it were, finds it too much when he sits down and writes that letter to the church at Ephesus. He keeps on diving off at different points. He starts a parenthesis in chapter three and gets so involved and so lost in glory that in the end, well we have gone on a different track all together in one sense, then we come back again. If you look at it, he says in Ephesians 4:1 "I therefore, the prisoner in the Lord, beseech you to walk worthily of the calling wherewith ye were called," In chapter two, he has got to the place where he says, "So then ye are no more strangers and sojourners, but ye are fellow-citizens with the saints, and of the household of God," that is verse 19. "Being built upon the foundation of the apostles and prophets, Christ Jesus himself being the chief corner stone; in whom each several building, fitly framed together, groweth into a holy temple in the Lord; in whom ye also are builded together for a habitation of God in the Spirit. For this cause I Paul, the prisoner of Christ Jesus in behalf of you Gentiles ..." (see Ephesians 2:19–3:1).

Then for the whole of the chapter, he dives off into, well off the deep end really, quite honestly, and he starts to talk about the mystery which has always been a headache for people ever since. He starts to talk about the mystery and his insight into the mysteries, his stewardship of mystery and the more you read it, it becomes colossal. He says in verse six, what is this mystery "to wit, that the Gentiles are fellow-heirs, and fellow-members of the body, and fellow-partakers of the promise in Christ Jesus through the gospel," and then he goes on and on. Then we come to this tremendous word in verse 20, "Now unto him that is able to do exceeding abundantly above all that we ask or think, according to the power that worketh in us, unto him be the glory in the church and in Christ Jesus ..." Then he puts the last bracket back, he finishes the parenthesis, he says, "I therefore, the prisoner in the Lord, beseech you to walk worthily of the calling wherewith ye were called ..." (Ephesians 4:1). Here is the calling. You are being called to be part of this corporate vessel which is for the glory of God, to contain and express the glory of God, throughout eternity. You know, dear friends, you and I, the redeemed of the Lord, we are as eternal as God because the Spirit of God has been given to us. We have been joined to our Lord Jesus Christ; we have become the body of which He is the head.

Glory in Eternity

You think of it. Eternity! What are we going to do through all eternity? What are our hands going to be filled with? What are our minds going to be filled with? It is not just going to be a kind of glorified hymn singing session. Some people get the idea from Revelation that it is just a kind of hymn singing session, you know, sort of forever and ever and ever. This just is not like God. I mean, God is not just interested in sort of a kind of enormous innumerable choir without end. Can you imagine it? No wonder agnostics and atheists smile at us, and say, "Well if that's their idea of God, well it is a bit odd isn't it? What kind of God is He that He just wants a kind of choir around Him the whole time for all eternity without end? We'll go to bed sort of saying, "Well, now tomorrow, we'll start again at nine o'clock."

So, what are we going to do? We don't really know. What we do know is this: that God is forming, a vessel for Himself with an objective that has not yet been revealed at a price that is simply beyond computation. We know that this world is a fallen world. Yet in it, we see so many things that are beautiful. We see something of the design rather like one of those ruined Roman buildings, or Greek buildings where we see something of the original idea but it is ruined. When we look at this universe, we see something of the original idea and yet it is in such a mess, that it is very difficult for us to determine exactly what it did look like, and what it was meant to be in the beginning. Sin has got into the very fabric of the universe, into every part of it. But you know, when this world is released from its bondage to corruption, when somehow it breaks the vicious circle that it has lived in for millenniums, then it will start to achieve what was God's original plan. We do not know what it is. What I am quite sure of is that God is God. God is a Person, if I may put it without seeming to be blasphemous. God is a Person. God is creative. God is not a machine.

Personally, I am quite sure that God has tremendous plans on foot. He has schemes which have been laid aside for millenniums because His chief creation, man, took the wrong path. You see, this vessel of glory we are talking about is the pivotal point of all that God is going to do in eternity to come, that city of God. Why does the Bible end with a city? The Bible ends with two things: a bride and a city. As I have often said, there are two ways of looking at marriage. One is that it is the end, and the other is that it is the beginning! There are two ways you can look at marriage. It is either the end or the beginning. Well I am sure most of us who are, I trust, more balanced, see it as the beginning. It is the beginning of something, the end of one phase in a relationship, the beginning of another. Isn't it rather beautiful that the Bible ends with the wedding of the church? Christ in the church? One phase is finished, now the eternal phase begins.

Glory in a City

What is a city? A city is, as it were, the centre of administration, the headquarters, as it were, the administration for a whole area, the centre of commerce, the centre of government, the centre, if you like, of national intercourse, that is a city. Why does the Bible take a city as its symbol and plant it right at the end of the last chapters of the Bible, doesn't it give us some glimpse into the future that this city is to be the centre of government, "They shall reign forever." "He shall sit down with Me in My throne," says the Lord. Some glimpse there of something lying beyond when the holy city, New Jerusalem becomes the centre point of all God's activity for eternity to come. Well, you see it is this city, which is the habitation of His glory. This house of God, this temple, however you like to look at it, this is the vessel of His glory. That is, if you and I would be part of it. Every one of us who has been born of God is potentially a member of the city. Every one of us who is born of God is potentially a member of the bride.

I personally do not believe that we shall all be there willy-nilly. I can only say with John Newton:

Saviour, if of Zion's city
I through grace a member am,
let the world deride or pity,
I will glory in Thy name

It is all grace, dear child of God, but it is the way you appropriate the grace that matters. God has made every one of us potentially part of that eternal city. He has given every one of us the potential to be part of the bride, and it is grace that shall get us there. But it is the way you and I appropriate the grace of God, and the provision made through that grace. He that overcometh shall inherit these things.

Let us look at a few scriptures now. Zechariah 2:5: "For I, saith the Lord, will be unto her," this is this city Jerusalem. If you look in verse four "a wall of fire round about, and I will be the glory in the midst of her." I will be the glory in the midst of her. Turn back to Haggai 2:7–9. Here is a great prophecy for the end of the age, "... and I will shake all nations; and the precious things of all nations shall come; and I will fill this house with glory, saith the Lord of hosts. The silver is mine, and the gold is mine, saith the Lord of hosts. The latter glory of this house shall be greater than the former, saith the Lord of hosts; and in this place will I give peace, saith the Lord of hosts." Turn back to the Psalms. Psalm 26:8, "Lord, I love the habitation of thy house, and the place where thy glory dwelleth." I love the habitation of Thy house, the home of Thy house. And the place where Thy glory dwelleth. Then, in Psalm 29:9, the last part of the verse says: "And in his temple everything saith, Glory." Everything, not just the part, but everything in His temple says, "Glory." There is not a single thing in that temple, in that house that does not manifest the glory of God and in the eternal building that the Holy Spirit is engaged in building. The house of God, the church of God, the bride of Christ, everything says, "Glory." In other words, in the temple, there is nothing that is not Christ. It is Christ wrought in us? It is Christ, as it were, increased in us. All the rest is outside. So my dear, dear friend, the more there is of you, your self-life in yourself, the less that is of glory. It is not in the house. Let us make no mistake about that. What is in the house is what there is of Christ, what the Spirit of God can produce of Christ in you and in me.

His Glory Dwelling

Now turn back even further to Exodus chapter 40. You remember how dear Moses prayed, "Show me Thy glory," in chapter 33, and how the Lord showed him His glory? He stood him on a rock, He put him into the cleft of the rock as the glory passed by and covered him with His hand. Now, just a few chapters later, we read this in Exodus 40:34–35. "Then the cloud covered the tent of meeting, and the glory of the Lord filled the tabernacle. And Moses was not able to enter into the tent of meeting, because the cloud abode thereon, and the glory of the Lord filled the tabernacle." Don't you think Moses thought back to what he prayed? "Show me I pray thee Thy glory." When he saw the glory of God personally, it was, as it were, just something that came and went. But this time, the glory of the Lord came and dwelt. It filled the tabernacle. You see, dear child of God, the point I am trying to make is that this matter of glory is, in its final analysis, corporate. If you turn to II Chronicles 5:13–14. "it came to pass, when the trumpeters and singers were as one, to make one sound to be heard in praising and thanking the Lord; and when they lifted up their voice with the trumpets and cymbals and instruments of music, and praised the Lord, saying, For he is good; for his lovingkindness endureth for ever; that then the house was filled with a cloud, even the house of the Lord, so that the priests could not stand to minister by reason of the cloud: for the glory of the Lord filled the house of God." This, of course, was the temple.

So when the tabernacle was set up, the very first time it was set up, the glory of God filled it. When the temple was set up for the first time and completed, at its dedication, the glory of the Lord filled it. It is just as if the Lord is saying all the way through, "This is the point. This is the objective. This is what I am driving at."

If you will also just look at II Chronicles 7:1, it is the same occasion. "Now when Solomon had made an end of praying, the fire came down from heaven, and consumed the burnt-offering and the sacrifices; and the glory of the Lord filled the house." Ezekiel 43:4–5: "And the glory of the Lord came into the house by the way of the gate whose prospect is toward the east. And the Spirit took me up, and brought me into the inner court; and, behold, the glory of the Lord filled the house." There you are. That is the great temple of Ezekiel, when finally Ezekiel saw it built and directed and completed, the glory of the Lord came and filled it.

Now turn to John 17. Listen, it is the same thing all over again. Starting in verse 21–22: "that they may all be one; even as thou, Father, art in me, and I in thee, that they also may be in us: that the world may believe that thou didst send me. And the glory which thou hast given me I have given unto them." Think about it! Just go away and think about it, and how could you not praise the Lord? Think! Think! How can the Lord say such a thing? "The glory which Thou, Father, has given Me I have given them the same glory." But He is without sin. He has perfectly fulfilled the Father's will. He has always done those things which were pleasing to Him. He has a right to glory.

In verse five, it says, "And now, Father, glorify thou me with thine own self." That is the best definition of glory. Listen to it again. And now, Father, glorify thou me with thine own self with the glory which I had with thee before the world was. Thyself! There you are. Glory. Glorify me with Thyself. Now the Lord turns it around and says, "The glory which Thou hast given Me I have given them." How can you and I receive the same glory as is due to the Lord Jesus Christ? How can you and I, worthless and vile sinners have the same glory? Think of it.

No wonder Paul nearly went spiritually berserk when he was writing letters. He was so filled with it, he saw so much, that he thought to himself, "My goodness me, how can I express it to them? These people dabbling in sin, these people cannot get on with each other colliding with each other over all these awful, silly, earthly, sensual problems they have got and look at them. They are the vessel for His glory." The glory which I have, which Thou hast given Me I have given them. You know, it is so wonderful to think of it.

When you want, you go away and really think about what I have said here in great meekness. It ought to do something for you because what it really means is this, that the Lord makes no distinction between the glory He is going to give you and the glory He Himself has got. Isn't that wonderful? He does not say, "Now look, I must have a glory that excels yours." The glory which is His, He has given to us. Exactly the same.

The Spirit and the Bride say, "Come"

Well, I think we must finish, and we will finish where we ought to finish with two references. Revelation 21:10–11: "And he carried me away in the Spirit to a mountain great and high, and showed me the holy city Jerusalem, coming down out of heaven from God, having the glory of God." Isn't that wonderful? Having the glory of God. Now look at verse 23, "And the city hath no need of the sun, neither of the moon, to shine upon it: for the glory of God did lighten it, and the lamp thereof is the Lamb." Isn't that interesting? You have got the lampstand again. The lamp is the Lamb. The light is the glory. The lampstand is the city. You are back again where we started. I have set before thee a lampstand all of gold. The glory. The lampstand, really, is to be the manifestation of the light of the glory of God in the face of Jesus Christ to all eternity. To all eternity.

No wonder the Spirit and the Bride say, "Come." Oh, are you going to be part of it? Am I going to be part of it? Can God get a capacity for glory in me? Can He get a capacity in you? Are we prepared to be built together, or are we going to 'play' church? Are we just going to quibble and squabble and fight and all the rest of it? Or sort of have wonderful conferences on biblical themes, and that is everything, and that is all? Is that what we are going to be? Or are we going to commit ourselves to the Lord so that He can do something in us, so deep, so thorough, that He can give it over to Antichrist, and when it has been outwardly and publicly destroyed, every bit of it has gone into the city. Every bit of it has gone into the city.

Don't you and I want to be part of that instead of these silly, little, woolly types of denominational things that collapse the moment the communist or any other "ism" comes. The history of China stands forever as a lesson to us all. They either collapsed in a heap as the Communists came in, or they went over and became communist party members and became a tool of communism, and for the destruction of faithful servants of the Lord. Shall we be like that? Surely not. We want to have something done so deeply in us; we want to be built so truly together. We want the Lord to knit us together so greatly, whatever the cost, whatever the price that the Lord can say, "I have done it. All right. Now come on Satan, you can have them. You can wreck them, you can destroy it all, you can take it away, you can make a play-thing of the whole thing for the valuable things have gone into heaven." Just like our Lord Jesus Christ, when in the garden of Gethsemane, He knew that it would be what was coming. The Father was going to hand Him over to Satan and He said, "Oh Father, if this cup can pass from Me, nevertheless not as I will but as Thou wilt." He went through. Why? Because the Lord had done such a work there. Christ had triumphed where everyone else had failed.

Well, the last reference without any further comment is Psalm 24. Now listen to this. We will not read the whole Psalm, you can read it because it has just actually put into words what I have said, but I am going to read from verse 7, "Lift up your heads, O ye gates; And be ye lifted up, ye everlasting doors: And the King of glory will come in. Who is the King of glory? The Lord strong and mighty, the Lord mighty in battle. Lift up your heads, O ye gates; Yea, lift them up, ye everlasting doors: And the King of glory will come in. Who is this King of glory? The Lord of hosts, He is the King of glory." Show me, I pray Thee, Thy glory.

Shall we pray?

Now Lord, we pray, that by Thy Holy Spirit, Thou wilst reveal to us the practical meaning and significance of Thy house and make us a people here and wherever else Thou has Thine own, a people ready at whatever the price, for Thee to work upon and in, in the light of our so great calling. We ask it in the name of our Lord Jesus. Amen.

4.
Seeing the Glory of God

Exodus 33:17–23

And the Lord said unto Moses, I will do this thing also that thou hast spoken; for thou hast found favor in my sight, and I know thee by name. And he said, Show me, I pray thee, thy glory. And he said, I will make all my goodness pass before thee, and will proclaim the name of Jehovah before thee; and I will be gracious to whom I will be gracious, and will show mercy on whom I will show mercy.

And he said, Thou canst not see my face; for man shall not see me and live. And the Lord said, Behold, there is a place by me, and thou shalt stand upon the rock: and it shall come to pass, while my glory passeth by, that I will put thee in a cleft of the rock, and will cover thee with my hand until I have passed by: and I will take away my hand, and thou shalt see my back; but my face shall not be seen.

Well, now, I cannot go back over all that we have said about glory. We have rambled, I think, through the whole Bible on the matter of glory. Yet, there was this portion that I really wanted to come back to and say something about. You remember, we started at this point: it was Moses' cry, "Show me Thy glory," which started us off on our ramble, as it were, through the Word of God. You will remember that I said Moses had previously had no small experience when he asked the Lord to show him His glory. Indeed, on at least two occasions, the glory of the Lord had appeared. Yet, Moses, after hearing His voice, seeing the fire of His presence, watching the finger of God carving out of the rock the ten commandments, the giving of the Law, the showing of the tabernacle (which was only a pattern of heavenly things) still asked this same question. Moses, after all that had happened before that in Egypt (the Passover, the exodus, the provision of the manna, the provision of water from the rock, the provision of quails, the pillar of cloud by day and the pillar of fire by night), after all these things that had happened to Moses, when he saw it again and again and again, these great acts of God, these great works of God, at the end of it all, his one great cry, torn out from the heart of the man, is this simple question: "Show me Thy glory, I pray."

Now, Moses must obviously have seen so much. As I have said to you before, if we had seen this, we should start to write our memoirs! It is not only common now with generals, and now this has happened amongst Christians too, to write their sort of memoirs. I am sure that if we had a third of the experiences of Moses, we would be writing all kinds of books like: "When I was Crossing the Red Sea," or "I was There at the Passover," or things like that. I mean, the fact of the matter is, we would be so contented, as I said before, we would probably found a Bible school on half of Moses' experience. We would be doing all kinds of things.

Yet, here is a man with an insatiable appetite. All that has come before has only done one thing—it has brought him to the heart of the matter. My dear friend, doesn't this really, in actual fact, make you and I feel small? Doesn't it make us feel finite, when sometimes we would give anything, to have just a few of the experiences of Moses? We feel that if we had them, that would be everything we need. This is only to find that the spiritual man can never be satisfied with things. Not even the works of God. The spiritual man, the hallmark of spiritual character, is an insatiable thirst for God Himself. With this thirst, even when we see the works of God, and we see the acts of God, when we are lost in the greatness of God and what He does, somehow or other, our satisfaction in these things falls away after a while. It is only the outskirts of His ways, the edges of His ways, and we know it. Some, of course, are content to stay there. That is the hallmark of the flesh in the things of God. However, when there is a spiritual character, even a small amount, then the hallmark of that character is a thirst for God Himself. God plays on that hunger and thirst. He develops it. He will give that man or that woman anything in order to develop that capacity for Himself, to bring the man to the place that Moses came to, where the cry of his heart was, "Show me Thy glory."

Now, you know that Moses had already just asked, I suppose, the most spiritual thing a person could ask for. He had said to the Lord, "Now, Lord, grant that Thy presence go with us." Isn't that enough? He said, "If Thy presence go not with us, we won't go." Now, that is a spiritual matter. That shows spiritual character, not to run before the Lord. Not to be carried along by our own momentum, even spiritually. Oh, it is so easy once the ball starts rolling, just to be carried forward by it, but Moses said, "No, if Thy presence doesn't go with us, we don't go." The Lord said to him, "My presence shall go with thee" (Exodus 33:14). The thought is, "My presence shall go and can carry you. It shall be in you and with you. I will give you rest."

Daily Renewal of the Inward Man

Now, it was immediately after this that Moses was not satisfied even with that. He says, "One more thing, Lord. Show me Thy glory," (Exodus 33:18). with an insatiable appetite for the Lord Himself. Well, now, we have said quite a lot about that already. We have been called unto His eternal glory. In Christ Jesus, I believe we have seen the light of the knowledge of the glory of God in the face of Jesus Christ which has shone into our hearts. Now, what I would like to ask is this: if that light of the knowledge of the glory of God in the face of Jesus Christ has shone into your heart and into my heart, is it producing an insatiable hunger and thirst for Himself and for that glory? You see, it is all a question of how we look at things. We can look at the Christian life as drudgery. We can look at the Christian life as just so much discipline. Oh, if we say, "I'm having the corners knocked off," then there is no joy in it. There is no glory in it. I am just having the corners knocked off. We can get the attitude of, "Well, the Christian life is just an endless routine, really. It is all tough going. It is all conflict and it is all this, that and the other," and we forget the word that we have in II Corinthians 4:16: "Wherefore we faint not; but though our outward man is decaying, yet our inward man is being renewed day by day."

Now, on the fact of our outward man decaying, we must make this point, that whether we are Christians or not, our outward man is decaying. That is a point that some Christians forget. They seem to think that it is part and parcel of the Christian life. They may think that it is nothing to do with the sort of decay of the physical body. Everyone is subject to that. That is our last great enemy called death, which one day will be abolished. You see, Paul says, "though our outward man is decaying, our inward man is being renewed." That is the point. Is it being renewed? Is it? That is where we have something the world has not got. The world has only an outward man. Its inward man is non-existent. So, all they can know is decay. The Christian may know an outward man decaying, but the inward man is being renewed day by day. There again is one of our little lessons: day by day.

Day by day. Some of us, go from convention to convention, or from conference to conference, or from highlight to highlight, but the Word of God says, "day by day." That is what you and I have got to learn: that it is finding the inward spring of eternal life in our own being that matters. We must learn to find it daily. There is a supply of the Spirit of Jesus, it is a daily supply. For some of us it may be only on Sundays, then gradually, we go down until we come back again. Yet, that is not good enough if we do not drink at the spring daily, if we do not appropriate what is ours daily.

Now, you who are young in the Lord, I will tell you: the secret of spiritual growth is daily appropriation. If you see something of Christ in anyone, you will know that it has come by appropriation. It will always be, to the end of time. If you find anyone who you feel is a windbag (putting it crudely), it is all up in the head and not in the heart. You will know there is no daily appropriation. Don't get worried about it. There will be windbags to the end of time! The Lord says in His Word, there must be factions amongst you so that the approved of God can be made manifest. The church is not a perfect place at all. It is a place where, like a laundry, everything is being washed. All the scum is coming to the surface. It is like a cutting out room. Everything is all over the place. All bits and pieces being thrown away by the tailor, while he is snipping out what he wants. That is the church.

I remember when I was younger, I heard it described as a pressure cooker. Once in, you could not get out! Well, I don't know about that, but unless you and I know the secret of daily appropriation, what will happen? Now, surely, there is not one of us who wants to be just an unwitting hypocrite. I believe there is not one person who wants to be a hypocrite. Yet, unwittingly, we become one. Why? It is because up in our heads we have got it, but deep down we have not. Why haven't we got it in there? It is because we are trying to get it second hand all the time. So, we go to this, we go to that, we go to the other and when we come into the orbit of power, or the orbit of a certain ministry, any ministry, ministry in this place or anywhere else, we are lifted up. But the moment we go out, we go down. It is not in us. It is not in us. It is coming from without, to us. When we get it—up we go. Then as soon as it stops, down we go. We have got to know what it means to be renewed day by day.

For an example, take the churches in the New Testament. If they had felt, "Now, we have to have the apostle Paul, for when he's with us, everything goes up," then what happens when he is in prison?! It all goes down. "He's on a chain. We can't get to it. So, we cannot get it. When we get a letter from him, it is not the same, you know? It is not the same, because Mr. So-and-So does not read it out in a right way. It is not like the apostle Paul. It is much nicer to have him with us because when he is with us, we feel power." You see? What happened when Paul was beheaded? Do you think half a million Christians lost their Christian life? Well, you see, the whole point is: where is the supply? Well, here the Word says, "... it is renewed day by day." Now read on, "... for our light affliction, which is for a moment, worketh for us ..." (v17) the affliction is doing something. It is not just an end, it is not just an affliction, but it is working for us, more and more exceedingly an eternal weight of glory. Glory! That is the point I wanted to get to.

You see, it is a question of how we look at a Christian life. It can be just a drudgery. It can be just like a class that we hate. We are being educated, we are being instructed, oh, but we hate it. We are just gritting our teeth, and we are going through. We don't really know why. We don't see the objective. We don't see what it is for. All we would like to do is to escape from it, if it were possible. But you see, the glory is essentially linked to the discipline of the Spirit of God, and to all these other things.

We Do not Know What We Ask

Now coming back to Exodus 33. Why is it that the Lord doesn't always answer our prayer? Why is it that when we say, "Show me, I pray Thee, Thy glory," the Lord doesn't hasten to show us His glory? There is a reason. You know, it is God's grace that the Lord answers our prayer when he says, "Yes." It is also God's grace when He answers our prayer and says, "No." This is because sometimes we do not know what we ask. Do you remember when the Lord said to the apostles, "Can you drink the cup that I drink? Can you be baptised with the baptism I am baptised with?" and they immediately said, "Yes"? He said, "You don't know what you ask." He then said, "You will drink the cup, and you will be baptised with the baptism that I am baptised with." But they did not know what they were asking. If it had been given to them at that point, they would have been completely finished (as Calvary revealed). They ran for their lives! They could not take it. All the way through, they had said, "Show us the Father." Again and again, they had said, "Show us Thy glory," but they could not take it. It was only after Pentecost, and after the deep, deep inward workings of the Spirit of God, that at long last those men were able to see the glory.

Now that is the same with you and me. We say, "Lord, I want to see Thy glory. Lord, I want You to commit Yourself to me." Do we know what we ask for? It is not just a baptism of the Spirit. It is a baptism of the Spirit and of fire. Do we know what we ask for? Well, now you see what the Lord said to Moses was very wonderful. He said, "No man has seen my face and lived," but look in verse 21 where the Lord said, "Behold, there is a place by Me." Isn't that beautiful? We could put it this way, the Father says to us, 'Behold, there is a place near to Me.' There is an old hymn that says, we are as near to God as we can be (I'm putting it in my own language) because we are in Christ. "There is a place by Me, there is a place near to Me." The only way a man can see the glory of God and live is in Christ. That is the only way.

The Foundation

There are three things. The first is this: the foundation. Look at it, "Thou shalt stand upon the rock." Why is it that the Lord cannot show you and me His glory sometimes? It is because we have not got the foundation under our feet. There is a lot of sand between our feet and the rock. You remember the two men who built their houses, one on the sand and one on the rock? When you read the Matthew 8 account (verses 24–27) it looks as if they just built two houses, one here and a few miles away another house. However, when you read the account in Luke 6:48–49, you find the two houses were side by side. One man built on the sand. The other man, "dug deep," it said, down to the rock underneath the sand, and built his house upon the rock.

Now, my dear friend, you and I can build on the subsoil of our own life. We can build on the subsoil, if you like, of our own flesh, of our own nature, of our old man. You can easily do that. There is no foundation. Those two houses appeared exactly alike. They were probably both clean, both quite sweet looking, both well cared for, both with nice curtains and all the rest of it looking as in a kind of Western contemporary way. Outwardly, they were perfect. They were the same. No one could see which one had the foundation till the storm came. The wind blew. The floods came. The house that was built on the rock stood. The house that was built on the topsoil of sand collapsed. Thou shalt stand upon the rock. What does God's Word say? Well, in 1 Corinthians 3:11, we read these words: "for other foundation can no man lay than that which is laid, which is Jesus Christ."

Now then, if you and I are going to have our prayer answered, our feet have got to be upon the rock of the Lord Jesus Christ. If you turn to Matthew 16:18, you know the well-known words of the Lord Jesus, "Thou art, Peter, upon this rock, I will build my church," the house of My glory, the place of My Glory, that is to be built upon the foundation, which is Jesus Christ. Not upon the topsoil of our own natures and gifts and talents and all the rest of it, but down through it all to the Foundation, which is the Lord Jesus Christ Himself. That, my dear friend, is a costly business and it is a laborious business.

Now, we all think we are on the foundation and so we are, if we take it as a general area. The question is, are our footings built on the rock? Let me put it another way, are our feet on the rock or on the sand above it? Which? You may have the most glorious superstructure, but when the flood comes, it sweeps it away, rock or no rock. You are on the rock, aha, true, but there is a yard or two of sand between you and the rock. When the storm comes and you say, "Show me, I pray Thee, Thy glory" the Lord replies "There is a place near to Me, thou shalt stand upon the rock." You know, if there had not been a spiritual lesson here, the Lord could have so easily said to Moses, "Stand over here. Stand over there." Why did he say, "Stand upon a rock?" This was because there was a lesson in it for us. If you and I are to see the glory of God, if we are to be changed from glory to glory, if there is an eternal weight of glory to be worked in us by our light affliction, our feet must be on the rock. We cannot bear the discipline of the Spirit of God. Yes, we will have the fullness and all the other things. We will have it all. But it is the discipline we won't have, and you cannot have the glory without the discipline. Therefore, the point is this, God cannot answer your prayer or my prayer until our feet are on the rock. Until we are prepared for the price of having our feet put upon the rock.

The foundation is given to us. Oh, let us be clear, God's grace has given us the foundation. There is no question about that. We cannot work for it; it has been given. One of these days, not so very far off, it is all going to be found out at the coming of the Lord. Suddenly, when we least expect it, the Lord will come. Then the houses built on the rock will stand and the houses on the sand will collapse. That is not the end of the story though because in the grace of God, the collapse of many Christians' superstructures will, in His mercy, bring many to put their feet on the rock. But why wait for such a shock? Why wait, until the time when everything is going to be shaken to pieces? Why wait? Why not even now stop to ask the Lord, "Lord, get my feet upon that foundation," remembering what Paul said in his very last letter to Timothy. There is a foundation, he said, "the foundation of God standeth fast having this seal, let him that nameth the name of the Lord depart from iniquity" (see II Timothy 2:19). Well, now that is one thing.

Hid in the Cleft

The second thing very swiftly you will find in Exodus 33 is that not only will you stand upon the rock, but "it shall come to pass while My glory passeth by I will put thee in a cleft of the rock." You know, you have got another wonderful picture there. If you and I are to know the glory of God, we must know our life hid with Christ in God. That is in Colossians 3:3 "for ye died, and your life is hid with Christ in God." We have got to know and experience Christ as our life. We have got to know what it is to have a hidden life—hid with Christ in God. In other words, it is not just an outward thing. Our Christian life is not our selves. It is Christ. It is the life of God in us.

If the Lord wants to change us from glory to glory, as we said before, there has not only got to be a discipline, there has got to be an experience. Our feet have to be down upon Christ Himself, upon His finished work and all that He is, upon all He has won for us, not our own works, but His. We have got to know Christ as our life, that we are hid with Christ in God. Do you know what it is to be crucified with Christ? Do you know what it is, really, to have died? Do you? Do I? You died and your life is hid with Christ in God. When Christ who is our life shall appear, then shall ye also appear with Him in glory. Do we know Him as our life? Christ in us is the hope of glory—I will hide thee in the cleft of the rock. If there is any flesh, there will be loss. Yet when you are hidden in Christ, covered with Christ, robed with Christ, and Christ is not only without, but within as well, there shall be glory.

Covered with His Hand

Do we know anything of that? "Show me, I pray Thee, Thy glory." The last thing is verse 22, "and I will cover thee with my hand." What an extraordinary thing. First, the Lord says, "You shall stand upon the rock," then He says, "I will put thee in the cleft of the rock so that you're hidden, and then I will put My hand over you, and cover you with My hand." The first thing is His foundation. The second thing is His life. The third thing is His protection. Do you and I realise that when we ask to see more of the Lord, when we ask for some deeper experience of Him, how we need to be covered? Do you realise that you and I are in enemy territory? Do we realise we are in a world that lieth in the evil one? Do we realise that there is one who is called the prince of the powers of the air, whose spirit worketh in the sons of disobedience? Do we realise it? Do we realise that every time you and I have more of Christ, every time we receive more of Him, every time He increases and I decrease, we are a marked people? We stand out from a mile away, spiritually. It is likened to when you look right around a huge congregation. I remember Billy Graham's meetings. I was amazed at the scarlet hats at his events. They stood out from a mile away. That vast sea of people's faces, some 20,000 people in that arena and you could pick out this and that colour. They were eye-catching. Now, when you and I have something of Christ, we are eye-catching as far as the devil goes. He spots us instantly. Not for us, but for Christ. "Huh! There is something of Christ there." Now, the moment there is more of Christ, you can be quite sure you will be tested.

When I was in Egypt there was a lady who we used to irreverently call, "Tiger." She was a lady who ran a big mission amongst soldiers, and she was the toughest lady I think I have ever seen, but a very dear Christian. I remember, I was a really young Christian and I once said to her, "Oh, the devil is busy. Blessing must be coming." and she looked at me and she said, "Hmmm, I suppose it is the way you look at it. I always say if the devil is busy, there has been a blessing." Well, it is a question of the way you look at it. It is true that if you have come into something more of the Lord, the fowls of the air are there immediately to snatch away what there is of God. So, you can be quite sure that every time you ask the Lord for something more, and in grace He brings you into it, the enemy is there to rob you of it. Then the end of that person can be worse than their beginning. We need covering.

Well, we must finish. If you get a chance, look in Ephesians 6 and see what it says in verse 11. It says, "Therefore, put on the whole armour of God." Covering. You know, it is something that you and I forget. We just forget. What is armour? It is covering. Covering! You see, if you are going to know Ephesians in experience, you have got to know the covering at the end. You have got to know what it is to have the helmet of salvation, the shield of faith, the breastplate of righteousness, the loins girt with truth, and the feet shod with the preparation of the gospel of peace—all these things. You have got to know them in experience, not just as theology and not just as doctrine. We have got to know how to take Christ for protection, for covering, so that every time we move into more of the Lord, we are covered. Don't we know it? Let us conclude with a look at Ephesians:

Finally, be strong in the Lord, and in the strength of his might. Put on the whole armor of God, that ye may be able to stand against the wiles of the devil. For our wrestling is not against flesh and blood, but against the principalities, against the powers, against the world-rulers of this darkness, against the spiritual hosts of wickedness in the heavenly places. Wherefore take up the whole armor of God, that ye may be able to withstand in the evil day, and, having done all, to stand. Stand therefore, having girded your loins with truth, and having put on the breastplate of righteousness, and having shod your feet with the preparation of the gospel of peace; withal taking up the shield of faith, wherewith ye shall be able to quench all the fiery darts of the evil one. And take the helmet of salvation, and the sword of the Spirit, which is the word of God: with all prayer and supplication praying at all seasons in the Spirit, and watching thereunto in all perseverance and supplication for all the saints, and on my behalf, that utterance may be given unto me in opening my mouth, to make known with boldness the mystery of the gospel, for which I am an ambassador in chains; that in it I may speak boldly, as I ought to speak.
Ephesians 6:10–20

Other books by Lance Lambert

For Zion's Sake

For Zion's sake, will I not hold my peace and for Jerusalem's sake, I will not rest until her righteousness go forth as brightness, and her salvation as a lamp, that burneth. Isaiah 62:1

Praise God. If we are so near to that coming of the Lord, the most obvious thing to do is to go through the gates, to commit oneself, to start this preparing of the way for the other people, to cast up the highway to gather out the stones. God help us. Thine eyes shall see the king in His beauty. Thou shalt see a land of far distances.

The Uniqueness of Israel

Woven into the fabric of Jewish existence there is an undeniable uniqueness. Israel's terrain, her history and chief city, all owe their uniqueness to the fact that God's appointed Saviour for the world was born a Jew. His destiny and theirs are forever intertwined. There is bitter controversy over the subject of Israel, but time itself will establish the truth about this nation's place in God's plan. For Lance Lambert, the Lord Jesus is the key that unlocks Jewish history He is the key not only to their fall, but also to their restoration. For in spite of the fact that they rejected Him, He has not rejected them.

The Eternal Purpose of God

With startling effect, Lance Lambert reveals the symmetrical design evident throughout the Bible, including the fascinating relationship between Genesis and Revelation. The author uncovers a dimension of the Bible that most believers will surely find a new revelation. The author writes,

> *"Why did God create this universe and this earth, which at our present extent of knowledge is unique? What was His aim and goal in its creation? Why did He create mankind? And when man fell short of His glory through sin, why did He persevere and provide salvation? Is that salvation an end in itself, or is it a means to an end, with everything provided within it to reach the final goal? And how can I be involved in the fulfillment of that purpose?"*

Through the Bible with Lance Lambert: Ezra, Nehemiah, Esther

Recovery. This key theme throughout the entire timeline of Ezra to Esther gives us a clear vision of the Lord's goal with His people. From the building of Jerusalem and its surrounding walls in Ezra and Nehemiah to the fixing of the irreversible decree of the annihilation of Jews in Esther, the Lord is constantly using His people for recovery. In this book of the series, "Through the Bible with Lance Lambert," we find an in depth analysis of Ezra, Nehemiah, and Esther, tracing the working of the Lord throughout history.

Find more books by Lance Lambert on lancelambert.org

"If Any Man Would Follow Me ..."

Battle for Israel

Be Ye Ready: Imperatives for Being Ready for Christ

Called Unto His Eternal Glory

Evangelism

Ezra - Nehemiah - Esther

Fellowship

For Zion's Sake

Gathering Together Volume 1: Christian Fellowship

Gathering Together Volume 2: Christian Testimony

God Wants a House

How the Bible Came to Be: Part 1

How the Bible Came to Be: Part 2

In the Day of Thy Power

Jacob I Have Loved

Lessons from the Life of Moses

Let the House of God Be Built: The Story and Testimony of Halford House

Living Faith

Love Divine

My House Shall Be a House of Prayer

Preparation for the Coming of the Lord

Qualities of God's Servants

Reigning with Christ
Spiritual Character
Talks with Leaders
The Battle of the Ages
The Eternal Purpose of God
The Glory of Thy People Israel
The Gospel of the Kingdom
The Importance of Covering
The Last Days and God's Priorities
The Prize
The Relevance of Biblical Prophecy
The Silent Years
The Supremacy of Jesus
The Uniqueness of Israel
The Way to the Eternal Purpose of God
They Shall Mount up with Wings
Thine Is the Power
Thou Art Mine
Through the Bible with Lance Lambert: Genesis - Deuteronomy
Till the Day Dawns
Unity : Behold How Good and How Pleasant - Ministries from Psalm 133
Warring the Good Warfare
What Is God Doing?: Lessons from Church History

www.ingramcontent.com/pod-product-compliance
Lightning Source LLC
Chambersburg PA
CBHW070546050426
42450CB00027B/3143